GLORIOUS GARLIC

COLE GROUP

Both U.S. and metric units are provided for all recipes in this book. Ingredients are listed with U.S. units on the left and metric units on the right. The metric quantities have been rounded for ease of use; as a result, in some recipes there may be a slight difference (approximately 1/2 ounce or 15 grams) between the portion sizes for the two types of measurements.

© 1995 Cole Group, Inc.

Front cover photograph: Kevin Sanchez

Cole Group
1330 N. Dutton Ave., Suite 103
Santa Rosa, CA 95401
(800) 959-2717   (707) 526-2682
Fax (707) 526-2687

Printed in Hong Kong

G F E D C B A
1 0 9 8 7 6 5

ISBN 1-56426-809-8

Library of Congress Catalog Card Number 95-16393

Distributed to the book trade by Publishers Group West

CONTENTS

THE GLORIES OF GARLIC

*G*ood cooks all over the world know that
simply the glorious aroma of garlic can
magically draw diners to the table, where the
heady fragrance heralds a flavorful, splendid
meal. Everywhere, garlic is minced, mashed,
chopped, braised, roasted, baked, marinated,
sautéed, fried, poached, pressed, pickled,
or preserved. Garlic is one herb that good
cooks everywhere keep on hand.

A LITTLE GOES A LONG WAY

With a simple clove of garlic, frugal and inventive cooks can transform their most humdrum and outdated dishes into fresh, new gourmet treasures. Inexpensive, plentiful all year round, with a shelf-life of months and a distinctive aroma that sets the mouth to watering, garlic is appreciated around the globe for its flavor, economy, and versatility.

If you have only loose change to spare on making an otherwise plain dinner memorable, spend it on one head of garlic and lavishly ply your family and guests with the heady herb. Cook up a beautiful garlic soup, rub garlic on meat, make a delicate sauce with it, put it in your favorite vinaigrette, or add it to homemade ice cream. After the meal, there may still be half a head of garlic left to produce yet another unforgettable feast.

WISDOM OF THE ANCIENTS

Probably originating in Asia, garlic has been of interest to humans since antiquity. First sought and hoarded for its curative properties, it was touted by Hippocrates as good for the digestion and for cleansing the body of toxins. During plagues, it was thought to ward off contagion, and by the Middle Ages, the crusaders, crisscrossing Europe and Asia, had begun to fine-tune it as a cooking herb. With the same purpose in mind as Mary Poppins, who insisted "a spoonful of sugar helps the medicine go down," cooks began to put the magical cloves in sauces and other dishes, making it easier to take. There was no going back from there.

Today, garlic is still claimed to be everything Hippocrates said it was and more. The humble clove has become the precious pearl, treasured both in the therapeutic and culinary arts.

Cultivating the Pungent Pearl

One of the beauties of garlic, a member of the lily family, is that it can be grown in most locales, its flowers making a pretty garden display. It thrives in the central coastal and valley regions of California, the premier garlic-producing state and supplier of 90 percent of all the garlic products marketed in the United States.

When the spear-shaped leaves turn brown, it's time for the bulbs to be dug up and dried. When the outer skin is thoroughly dried, it will be thin like parchment paper and easily crushed, allowing the head to be readily opened to expose the cloves nestled inside.

After drying, store the heads of garlic in a cool, dry, airy place. Depending on the variety and storage conditions, a string of these pungent pearls can last for months. Once the head is opened, however, the cloves rapidly dry out.

Individual cloves might be encased in either a translucent white, pink, or purplish sheath, depending on the variety. Each head will contain from 12 to 16 pearly cloves. In selecting garlic, avoid heads that are withered or flecked with brown spots or mold, or cloves that show signs of sprouting or softening.

RELEASING GARLIC'S MAGIC

Properly prepared, garlic can work pure magic, enlivening food and bringing out the best in other ingredients. The amount of flavor a clove of garlic releases depends on how it is prepared—peeled and left whole, chopped, minced, or crushed—and whether and how it is cooked. Crushed raw, garlic is at its most potent; slow-roasted, garlic develops a delicate, sweet flavor. To prepare an unpeeled clove for cooking, mash the clove gently with the flat side of a knife blade to loosen the skin; to crush the clove, hit the knife blade repeatedly until the clove begins to release some of its oil. The clove can then be added to other ingredients or put inside a piece of cheesecloth or muslin if the recipe calls for removing the garlic before serving the finished dish.

Most recipes call for the cloves to be peeled. If the peeled clove is to be used whole, mash the clove lightly with the flat side of a knife to loosen the skin, or gently peel the skin with a knife, beginning the process by trimming the root end. If the recipe calls for the clove to be chopped or minced, first press the clove with the flat side of the knife. Then remove the skin, slice the clove several times lengthwise, and mince or coarsely chop at a right angle to the first cuts. Pressing a clove in a garlic press can be done with the skin intact or removed.

To peel a large number, separate cloves from the head, rub the skins in oil, put inside cheesecloth or a towel, and place in the sun for several hours. Then remove the skins by rubbing the cloves together inside the cheesecloth. Or microwave the cloves for 15–20 seconds or blanch them in boiling water to loosen the skins.

THE ALCHEMY OF GARLIC

Raw, preserved, or cooked, garlic possesses an alchemical quality that gives it perpetual appeal. Raw garlic rubbed through a sieve can be used to season salads or vegetables. As a rub for meat, poultry, or fish that is to be baked or barbecued, raw garlic lends flavorful but subtle character. Pressed, crushed or ground, raw garlic can be folded into butter or mayonnaise to make a delicious spread.

Fresh garlic can easily be stored for later use. When peeled, cloves of garlic can be frozen or preserved in the refrigerator in covered jars for several weeks. Crushed cloves can be put in a jar and then easily dished out by the teaspoonful for sauces, soups, and spreads. Garlic cloves can also be pickled in vinegar or preserved in oil.

Cooked, garlic has even more potential. Baked whole in the oven or grilled, it becomes a sweet, buttery spread for bread or potatoes. Braised or simmered, it enhances stews, soups, and one-pot dishes. Sautéed garlic transforms plain sauces into haute cuisine. With plenty of garlic on hand, the culinary possibilities are as delightful as they are endless.

RECIPES AND TECHNIQUES FOR GLORIOUS GARLIC

Garlic glorifies any meal. In this section you will find not only delectable, irresistible recipes for garlic-infused fare, but techniques for storing, preparing, baking, roasting, and cooking with the versatile clove. Among the recipes sure to win acclaim from garlic aficionados are Marinated Goat Cheese (see page 18), Sweet Garlic Potage With Rouille (see page 34), Chicken Ali Baba (see page 64), and Stinking Rose Ice Cream (see page 93).

First Courses
and
Accompaniments

The richly pungent aroma and savory flavor of garlic needn't be reserved for the entrée. As a precursor to the main event, garlic stimulates the appetite and pleases the palate. From dips, breads, and soups to salads, sauces, and vegetables, the recipes on the following pages demonstrate the power of garlic to introduce zest and intensity into a variety of foods.

THAI PORK BALLS WITH
RICE STICK NOODLES

The Thai fish sauce and rice stick noodles for these spicy meatballs are available in Asian markets.

Dipping Sauce

2 cups each	white vinegar and sugar	500 ml each
1 tbl	salt	1 tbl
6 cloves	garlic, minced	6 cloves
8	fresh hot red chiles, seeded and finely sliced	8
1 lb	lean ground pork	450 g
1 tbl	minced garlic	1 tbl
1 tbl	freshly ground black pepper	1 tbl
1 tsp	salt	1 tsp
¼ cup	Thai fish sauce	60 ml
3–4 oz	rice stick noodles	85–115 g
2	eggs, lightly beaten	2
as needed	peanut oil, for deep-frying	as needed

1. To prepare Dipping Sauce, combine vinegar, sugar, salt, garlic, and chiles in a saucepan. Bring to a boil, stirring. Remove from heat and let cool at room temperature. Set aside.

2. In a bowl mix together pork, garlic, pepper, salt, and Thai fish sauce. Shape into 12 small balls.

3. Cook noodles 1½ minutes in large volume of boiling salted water; drain and rinse under cold water.

4. Dip each pork ball into beaten eggs, then wrap in boiled noodles, pressing firmly to make noodles adhere. Heat oil in a deep skillet or wok to 375°F (190°C). Fry balls a few at a time until they are crisp and browned. Drain on paper towels, then serve with Dipping Sauce.

Makes 12 cocktail meatballs.

CAMBODIAN RED CURRY PASTE

The generous quantity of garlic in this authentic Cambodian curry paste gives singular potency to any dish in which it is used (see below). Galangal (a member of the ginger family), Kaffir lime peel, and shrimp paste are available in most Asian markets.

2	dried California or New Mexico chiles	2
2 stalks	lemongrass, thinly sliced	2 stalks
1 head	garlic, separated into cloves and peeled	1 head
3 slices	fresh galangal, minced	3 slices
8 strips	Kaffir lime peel, soaked, drained, and minced	8 strips
1 tsp	salt	1 tsp
1 tsp	shrimp paste	1 tsp
1 tsp	ground coriander	1 tsp
½ tsp	ground cumin	½ tsp

1. Split chiles down the side and remove seeds and veins. Tear flesh into small pieces and soak in warm water until soft. Drain.

2. Combine chiles, lemongrass, garlic, galangal, lime peel, salt, and shrimp paste in a mortar and pound to a paste. Add ground spices and combine. Cover and refrigerate until ready to use.

Makes ⅓ cup.

COOKING WITH CURRY PASTE

Using a prepared curry paste, you can put together a tasty curry of meat, poultry, fish, or vegetables that's ready in less time than it takes to cook the rice that will accompany the curried dish. Heat a can of coconut milk in a wok, add a tablespoon or two of curry paste, and cook until fragrant. Add two teaspoons of fish sauce and simmer until the aroma of the fish sauce dissipates and the mixture is slightly thickened. Serve over rice.

CHILES AND GARLIC IN OIL

This simple yet powerful spread is good served as a starter with French bread. The fiery combination of soft chiles, onion, and garlic is sure to ignite your taste buds. For a daring dining experience, begin your meal with this recipe and end with Stinking Rose Ice Cream (see page 93).

2	red bell peppers, seeded, stems intact	2
6	fresh hot chiles (preferably a mixture of red, green, and yellow), seeded, stems intact	6
3	fresh Anaheim or poblano chiles, seeded, stems intact	3
6	boiling onions, peeled	6
20 cloves	garlic, peeled	20 cloves
1	onion, cut into ½-inch (1.25-cm) rings	1
1 bundle	fresh dill, tied together	1 bundle
as needed	olive oil	as needed

1. Place all vegetables in a large skillet with a tight-fitting lid. Place dill atop vegetables and pour in enough olive oil to stand 1 inch (2.5 cm) deep in pan.

2. Over moderate heat, slowly bring oil to a simmer, then reduce heat to very low. Remove dill, turn vegetables, then return dill to skillet.

3. Cover and simmer for 45 minutes, or until boiling onions are soft. Remove from heat and leave covered until cool. Remove dill before serving.

Serves 6.

SUNLESS DRIED TOMATOES WITH GARLIC

Tomatoes dried in an oven or dehydrator instead of in the sun retain their fresh, bright color. The dried tomatoes packed in oil will keep at room temperature for two to three months. Refrigerate for longer storage. Serve these garlic-permeated tomatoes on cocktail picks as an appetizer, chop them into salads, toss them with pasta, or use them to top pizza.

3 lb	fresh Roma or other small paste tomatoes	1.4 kg
to taste	salt	to taste
3 cloves	garlic, peeled	3 cloves
2–3 sprigs	rosemary	2–3 sprigs
as needed	olive oil	as needed

1. Slice tomatoes lengthwise almost in half and lay them open like a book (cut side up). Sprinkle cut surfaces lightly with salt.

2. Place tomatoes, cut side up, on drying trays. Dry in a dehydrator or the oven at 120°F–140°F (49°C–60°C): 4 hours or longer in a dehydrator, or 24 hours or longer in the oven. When tomatoes are dry, they will be shriveled to small, flattish ovals and will feel dry but still pliable, not brittle.

3. Pack tomatoes, garlic, and rosemary loosely into 2 or 3 half-pint (250-ml) jars. Pour in enough oil to cover tomatoes completely—they may mold if exposed to air. Cap jars.

4. Let stand in a cool, dark place for 1 month for flavors to develop.

Makes 2 half pints (500 ml).

MARINATED GOAT CHEESE

This garlic-infused appetizer originates in the antipasto platters of northern Italy. Marinated Goat Cheese can be served on a bed of lettuce and radicchio or spread on French bread or crisp rye crackers. The green olive oil used in this recipe is made from unripe olives; it can be found in specialty food markets or in the gourmet aisle of most supermarkets.

10 cloves	garlic, thinly sliced	10 cloves
⅓ cup	extra virgin olive oil	85 ml
¼ cup	green olive oil	60 ml
¼ cup	Niçoise or Greek olives, pitted	60 ml
pinch	freshly ground black pepper	pinch
1 tsp	dried thyme	1 tsp
1 tsp	dried oregano	1 tsp
1 tsp	dried tarragon	1 tsp
½ lb	goat cheese	225 g
as needed	lettuce leaves for lining platter	as needed
as needed	olives, peeled garlic cloves, or fresh herbs, for garnish	as needed

1. In a heavy skillet over medium heat, sauté garlic slices in olive oils until slightly golden. Remove skillet from heat.

2. Add olives, pepper, thyme, oregano, and tarragon to garlic and oil mixture.

3. Cut goat cheese into 1½-inch (3.75-cm) pieces. Lay pieces in a flat-bottomed casserole. Pour garlic and oil mixture over cheese and cover with plastic wrap. Let marinate for 24–48 hours in the refrigerator before serving.

4. To serve, arrange cheese on lettuce. Garnish with olives, garlic, or herbs.

Serves 8.

ROASTED GARLIC

Roasted garlic is nutty and sweet, with the texture of butter. If you don't have access to a grill, try baking garlic. Prepare the heads as you would for roasting, then bake them in a preheated 325°F (160°C) oven for 1 hour and 15 minutes. Partially open the foil packet, bake for an additional 15 minutes, and then serve. Don't discard any of the olive oil-and-butter mixture remaining in the foil packets; it is delicious drizzled over French bread. You can roast or bake garlic without using aluminum foil, but you will lose some of the flavorful cooking juices.

6 heads	garlic	6 heads
¼ cup	olive oil	60 ml
4 tbl	unsalted butter	4 tbl
4 sprigs	fresh oregano	4 sprigs

1. Prepare fire for indirect-heat method of cooking (place a drip pan underneath rack, with coals heaped around sides of pan). Cut the top end off the garlic heads, exposing the individual garlic cloves in their skins. Place the heads in a piece of heavy-duty aluminum foil and drizzle with olive oil. Dot with butter and lay oregano on top. Tightly seal aluminum foil to form a packet. Place on grill in a spot not directly over the coals.

2. After 45 minutes, open packet (be careful of escaping steam) and baste heads with butter-oil mixture from bottom of packet. Reseal and continue to cook until garlic is spreadably soft (about 45 minutes more). Remove packet from grill and open carefully, reserving any butter-oil mixture for drizzling over bread or other foods.

Serves 4 to 6.

NEAPOLITAN GARLIC TOAST

This peppery version of French toast is an excellent complement to a soup or stew. Thick slices of egg-dipped bread are seasoned with garlic, pepper, and fennel seed, then topped with Parmesan cheese and baked until golden.

as needed	olive oil	as needed
1 tbl	minced garlic	1 tbl
1 tbl	fennel seed, lightly crushed in a mortar	1 tbl
1 tbl	freshly ground black pepper	1 tbl
1 tsp	salt	1 tsp
5	eggs	5
1 loaf	Italian bread, unsliced	1 loaf
2 tbl	freshly grated Parmesan cheese	2 tbl

1. Preheat oven to 350°F (175°C). Lightly oil a large baking sheet. Combine garlic, fennel seed, pepper, and salt in a small bowl and set aside.

2. Cut bread into ¾-inch (1.9-cm) slices. Whisk together eggs and 3 tablespoons olive oil. Dip bread slices in egg mixture one at a time and let them soak briefly to absorb some egg. Arrange bread slices on baking sheet.

3. Dust bread slices with half the garlic mixture. Bake 10 minutes. Turn slices, dust with remaining garlic mixture, and bake 10 minutes. Sprinkle with cheese and bake an additional 5 minutes, or until bread is golden. Serve hot.

Makes 12 slices.

Anchoiade

A smooth and pungent spread popular in southern France and Corsica, anchoiade can be slathered on toasted French bread, pizza dough, and breadsticks. It keeps, refrigerated, for up to three weeks and can be served with cocktails or a dry white wine.

6 cans (2 oz each)	anchovies	6 cans (60 ml each)
3 cloves	garlic, minced	3 cloves
½ cup	minced parsley	125 ml
3	egg yolks	3
1½ cups	fresh bread crumbs	350 ml
¼ cup	red wine vinegar	60 ml
¾ cup	extra virgin olive oil	175 ml
1 tbl	minced fresh thyme	1 tbl

1. In a blender combine anchovies with their oil, garlic, parsley, and egg yolks. Blend well. Add bread crumbs and blend. Mixture will be a thick paste. Add red wine vinegar and blend.

2. With blender on low speed, add olive oil drop by drop. Mixture will mount like a mayonnaise. Transfer Anchoiade to a bowl and stir in fresh thyme.

Makes about 3 cups (700 ml).

Making Garlic Oil

Simple to make and useful to keep on hand, garlic oil can enliven pasta, pizza, salad dressings, breads, vegetables, meats, fish, and poultry. To make garlic oil, add 6 whole peeled garlic cloves to 1 pint (500 ml) extra virgin olive oil. Let stand in a tightly capped glass or ceramic container in a cool, dark place for 1 week before using. Garlic oil will keep indefinitely if covered and refrigerated.

FOCACCIA WITH SWEET GARLIC PEARLS

Garlic purée pervades every crumb of this Italian bread.

¼ cup	olive oil	60 ml
12 cloves	garlic, peeled	12 cloves
½ cup	slightly sweet white wine	125 ml
2 pkg (2 tbl)	active dry yeast	2 pkg (2 tbl)
½ cup	warm water (about 105°F or 41°C)	125 ml
3 cups	flour	700 ml
1 cup	warm milk	250 ml
¼ cup	freshly grated Parmesan cheese	60 ml
½ cup	finely minced parsley	125 ml
to taste	freshly ground black pepper	to taste

1. In a saucepan heat oil. Add garlic and cook over moderately high heat for 5 minutes. Reduce to low; add wine. Cook gently until most of wine has evaporated (about 30 minutes). Remove from heat and reserve 6 garlic cloves. Mash remaining cloves. Set aside.

2. To prepare dough, dissolve yeast in the water and let proof 5 minutes. Put 1 cup (250 ml) flour in a bowl and slowly add yeast mixture. Beat well; cover and set aside in a warm place for 1 hour. When dough has risen, stir in mashed garlic and remaining 2 cups (500 ml) flour, then slowly incorporate the warm milk. Beat well, cover again, and let rise in a warm place for 45 minutes.

3. Preheat oven to 400°F (205°C). Oil a baking sheet and pour in the dough—it will be soupy. Slice the reserved garlic; sprinkle over dough. Dust surface with cheese, parsley, and pepper. Bake until browned, about 35 minutes. Remove from pan; cool 10 minutes before cutting.

Makes 16 squares.

WATERCRESS DIP WITH GARLIC AND BASIL

This dip is a showstopper—a nutty, coarse-textured creation fragrant with garlic and brilliantly green. Arrange a basket of crudités beside it: cherry tomatoes, cauliflower and broccoli florets, snow peas, endive leaves, zucchini and carrot spears, artichoke hearts, radishes, or fennel. The dip keeps up to 10 days, refrigerated.

3 cups	watercress, stems trimmed	700 ml
¾ cup	fresh basil leaves	175 ml
¼ cup	minced garlic	60 ml
½ cup	extra virgin olive oil	125 ml
1 cup	freshly grated Parmesan cheese	250 ml
¾ cup	whipping cream	175 ml
½ cup	finely ground walnuts	125 ml
¼ cup	minced green onions	60 ml
to taste	salt and freshly ground black pepper	to taste
1 tbl	milk or water (optional)	1 tbl

1. In a blender combine watercress, basil, garlic, olive oil, and cheese. Blend to a paste. Add cream and blend only until mixed; do not overblend.

2. Transfer mixture to a bowl and stir in walnuts and green onion. Add salt and pepper to taste. Mixture will thicken as it stands; if desired, add a tablespoon of milk or water to thin it slightly before serving.

Makes 2 cups (500 ml).

CREAM CHEESE-GARLIC DIP WITH PITA TOASTS

This rich, garlicky dip goes as well with a platter of crudités as with these crunchy pita toasts. Serve the dip in a hollowed-out red or green bell pepper for an elegant presentation.

8 oz	cream cheese	225 g
2 tbl	mayonnaise	2 tbl
½	lemon, juiced	½
3 cloves	garlic, pressed	3 cloves
¼	onion, finely minced	¼
1 tsp	dried dill	1 tsp
1 tsp	salt	1 tsp
to taste	hot-pepper sauce	to taste
1	red bell pepper	1

Pita Toasts

3 rounds	pita bread	3 rounds
1 tsp	garlic powder	1 tsp

1. In a small bowl, mix together cream cheese, mayonnaise, lemon juice, garlic, onion, dill, and salt. Add hot-pepper sauce to taste. Cut top off bell pepper and remove seeds. Spoon dip into hollowed-out bell pepper, cover with plastic wrap, and chill until shortly before serving time.

2. Cut each round of pita bread into 4 equal wedges. Toast until crisp, then dust lightly with garlic powder. Arrange on a platter with dip.

Serves 12.

GARLIC AND LEEK TARTLETS

Braised leeks combined with a purée of garlic make an unusual filling for these miniature tarts.

2 heads	garlic, separated into cloves	2 heads
1 cup	water	250 ml
1⅓ cups	whipping cream	335 ml
½ cup	butter, softened	125 ml
3–4	leeks, thinly sliced	3–4
to taste	salt and freshly ground black pepper	to taste
4	egg yolks	4
24	partially baked 2-inch (5-cm) tartlet shells	24
⅓ cup	freshly grated Parmesan cheese	85 ml

1. Peel garlic cloves and combine in a saucepan with water and 1 cup (250 ml) of the cream. Bring to a boil, then reduce heat and simmer very slowly until garlic is tender (about 1 hour).

2. Purée softened garlic in a food processor or blender. Transfer to a bowl and stir in 2 tablespoons softened butter.

3. Preheat oven to 375°F (190°C). In a large skillet, melt remaining butter. Add leeks, salt, and pepper, and cook over moderate heat, stirring occasionally, until leeks are quite tender (about 20 minutes). Add remaining cream and continue cooking until mixture is thick and creamy. Remove from heat.

4. Combine leeks and puréed garlic. Add egg yolks and mix well.

5. Distribute filling among tartlet shells. Dust tarts lightly with cheese, then place on a heavy baking sheet and bake until browned and slightly puffed (about 10–12 minutes). Cool briefly before serving.

Makes 24 tartlets.

Preparing Garlic

Carefully separate individual cloves from the garlic head and remove outer husk. For the best flavor, use the cloves within a few weeks after separating them. If any cloves show evidence of sprouting—which can give garlic a bitter taste—halve the cloves lengthwise and remove the sprouting core. Use a paring knife to remove any dark or soft areas.

Although a garlic press is a favorite tool of many cooks, it causes the cell walls of the clove to collapse in a way that yields a sharper, stronger flavor than that of garlic that has been crushed, chopped, or minced with a knife. Try both methods and use the one that produces the flavor and texture you like best.

1. To loosen skin, put garlic clove on a board. Rest the flat side of a large-bladed knife on the clove and lightly pound blade with heel of hand or side of fist until skin loosens. Peel skin from clove.

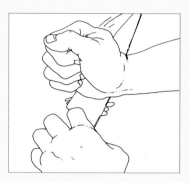

2. To crush garlic, place peeled garlic on board and position knife above it as in Step 1. Hit blade vigorously with heel of hand or side of fist until garlic is crushed to the desired consistency.

3. To chop garlic, slice the peeled clove several times lengthwise, then chop at right angles to the first cuts. To mince garlic, chop until pieces are uniformly fine.

SPANISH GARLIC SOUP

Eight cloves of garlic enrich this flavorful soup.

8 thin slices	French baguette	8 thin slices
1 tbl	butter	1 tbl
1½ tbl	olive oil	1½ tbl
pinch	cayenne pepper	pinch
8 cloves	garlic, sliced	8 cloves
1 tbl	tomato paste	1 tbl
2 cans (15 oz each)	beef stock	2 cans (450 ml)
½ cup	dry sherry	125 ml
to taste	salt and freshly ground black pepper	to taste
4	eggs, poached	4
3 slices	bacon, cooked and crumbled	3 slices
as needed	cilantro (coriander leaves), for garnish	as needed

1. To prepare croutons, preheat oven to 300°F (150°C). Place baguette slices on a baking sheet. Melt butter with ½ tablespoon oil; stir in cayenne pepper. Brush butter mixture over bread slices. Bake until crisp (20 minutes). Reheat before serving soup.

2. In a heavy saucepan, heat remaining olive oil over medium heat. Add garlic and cook until lightly browned. Dilute tomato paste with a little of the stock; add with remaining stock to garlic mixture. Bring to a boil, cover, reduce heat, and simmer for 20 minutes.

3. Remove garlic from stock; discard garlic. Add sherry to stock. Season with salt and pepper to taste. Reheat until stock begins to boil.

4. To serve, place 2 hot croutons into each of 4 warm soup bowls. Put a poached egg into each bowl on top of croutons. Pour hot soup over eggs. Sprinkle each serving with bacon and cilantro.

Serves 4.

GARLIC SOUP GILROY-STYLE

Gilroy, located east of Santa Cruz, California, is the self-proclaimed "Garlic Capital" of the world. Each year the town conducts a harvest festival that fills the air with the aroma of garlic being prepared in dozens of ways. This Gilroy recipe simmers the hometown specialty to bring out its sweetness.

1 tsp	olive oil	1 tsp
1 cup	dry white wine	250 ml
1	onion, finely chopped	1
5 heads	garlic, wrapped in cheesecloth and mashed	5 heads
4 cups	chicken stock	900 ml
2	bay leaves, crushed	2
½ tsp	dried thyme	½ tsp
¼ tsp	dried marjoram	¼ tsp
4 sprigs	parsley, chopped	4 sprigs
to taste	salt and freshly ground black pepper	to taste
½ cup	milk	125 ml

1. In a stockpot heat oil and wine; add onion and sauté over medium heat until onion is soft.

2. Add garlic wrapped in cheesecloth, stock, bay leaves, thyme, marjoram, and parsley. Bring to a boil; lower heat, cover, and simmer for 45 minutes. (Do not let soup boil rapidly or garlic will become bitter.)

3. Remove cheesecloth packet of garlic. Take soft, cooked garlic from cloth and force it through a sieve, leaving the papery skins behind; add sieved garlic to soup.

4. Add salt, pepper, and milk; heat through and serve.

Serves 6.

Allium Bisque

Alliums include garlic, chives, leeks, onions, and shallots.

2 tbl each	butter and olive oil	2 tbl each
4	onions, diced	4
10 cloves	garlic, minced	10 cloves
4	shallots, minced	4
4	leeks, cut into ¼-inch (.6-cm) slices	4
4	potatoes, peeled and cut into ½-inch (1.25-cm) cubes	4
6 cups	vegetable stock	1.4 l
2 tsp	salt	2 tsp
1 tsp	dried basil	1 tsp
1	bay leaf	1
1 tsp	dried oregano	1 tsp
½ tsp	dried marjoram	½ tsp
as needed	minced chives, for garnish	as needed

1. In a saucepan, heat butter and oil. Add onions, garlic, shallots, and leeks. Cook slowly over low heat until lightly browned. Add potatoes, vegetable stock, salt, basil, bay leaf, oregano, and marjoram.

2. Bring to a boil, reduce heat to simmer, and cook for 40 minutes. Serve immediately or refrigerate and reheat before serving. Garnish with minced chives.

Serves 6.

Storing Garlic

Keep fresh garlic in a cool, dry, dark place with some air circulation, such as a ventilated cabinet or a mesh bag—not in a plastic bag or airtight container. Keep dried garlic flakes and garlic powder in tightly sealed glass containers and store them in a cool, dry, dark place. These products have a shelf life of only about six months.

SWEET GARLIC POTAGE WITH ROUILLE

A spicy pepper and almond spread tops the croutons that float on this thick garlic soup of French descent.

Rouille

1	red bell pepper	1
¼ cup	almonds	60 ml
1 clove	garlic	1 clove
1	egg yolk	1
¼ tsp	cayenne pepper	¼ tsp
½ tsp	salt	½ tsp
2 tbl	olive oil	2 tbl
8 heads	garlic	8 heads
10 cups	vegetable stock	2.3 l
1 tbl	salt	1 tbl
1	French baguette	1
as needed	parsley, for garnish	as needed

1. To prepare Rouille, roast, peel, and seed red pepper. Place pepper in food processor or blender with almonds, garlic, egg yolk, cayenne, and salt. With food processor or blender running, add oil in a thin stream until purée thickens. Set aside.

2. Separate garlic cloves, leaving skins intact. In a saucepan, bring vegetable stock to a boil. Add garlic cloves and salt. Reduce heat and simmer 45 minutes.

3. Place a food mill over a 3-quart (2.7-l) bowl. Place some of the cooked garlic cloves into the food mill with the stock. Purée garlic. Repeat with remaining garlic and stock.

4. Slice baguette, toast, and spread with Rouille. Serve soup in shallow bowls with a Rouille-covered crouton floating on top. Sprinkle with parsley.

Serves 4.

BOURRIDE

Aioli and Garlic Croutons complement this fish soup.

5 cups	fish or chicken stock	1.1 l
1 cup	dry white wine	250 ml
1 tsp	orange zest	1 tsp
½ tsp	dried thyme	½ tsp
3	bay leaves	3
1 tsp	freshly ground black pepper	1 tsp
1 tsp	fennel seed	1 tsp
to taste	salt	to taste
2½ lb	cod fillets cut into 1½-inch (3.75-cm) cubes	1.2 kg
1 recipe	Aioli (see page 38)	1 recipe
as needed	Garlic Croutons (see page 44)	as needed
3 tbl	minced chives, for garnish	3 tbl

1. In a stockpot over moderate heat, combine stock, wine, orange zest, thyme, bay leaves, pepper, and fennel seed. Simmer and cook for 15 minutes. Strain into a clean pot. Season to taste with salt.

2. Return stock to a simmer over moderate heat. Add cod and cook until fish begins to flake (3–4 minutes). Remove fish to a warm platter. Moisten with ¼ cup (60 ml) stock, cover, and keep in a low oven.

3. Put 1 cup (250 ml) of the Aioli in a bowl. Whisk in ½ cup (125 ml) hot stock. Whisk this mixture back into stockpot. Cook over low heat, stirring constantly with a wooden spoon, until visibly thickened (about 3 minutes). Do not allow soup to boil or it will curdle.

4. To serve, place 2–3 croutons in each of 6 warm soup bowls. Put a few cubes of fish in each bowl. Ladle stock into bowls. Garnish with minced chives. Pass any extra croutons and the remaining Aioli separately.

Serves 6.

AIOLI

This classic Provençale sauce—actually a garlic-flavored mayonnaise—can be the focus of a light meal if accompanied by cooked vegetables and a crusty French baguette. Aioli is a wonderful sauce for grilled fish as well and is traditionally served with Bourride (see page 36). If you are too short on time to make Aioli from scratch, add 3 to 6 cloves crushed garlic to 1 cup (250 ml) bottled mayonnaise and blend well before serving.

1½ tbl	coarsely chopped garlic	1½ tbl
1 tsp	salt, plus salt to taste	1 tsp
3	egg yolks	3
1½ cups	olive oil	350 ml
as needed	lemon juice	as needed

1. In a food processor, process garlic, salt, and yolks until smooth. With motor running, begin adding oil drop by drop through feed tube. When mixture is thick and smooth, add remaining oil in a thin stream.

2. Transfer to a bowl and season to taste with lemon juice, adding more salt if necessary. Serve at once or refrigerate for up to 24 hours.

Makes 2 cups (500 ml).

AUTUMN BROCCOLI SALAD

Mustard, garlic oil, and Parmesan cheese flavor the dressing for this simple salad.

1 tsp	mustard	1 tsp
2 tbl	red wine vinegar	2 tbl
2 tsp	lemon juice	2 tsp
½ cup	garlic oil (see Making Garlic Oil on page 22)	125 ml
½ cup	freshly grated Parmesan cheese	125 ml
to taste	salt and freshly ground black pepper	to taste
4 cups	broccoli florets	900 ml
2 cups	cherry tomatoes, halved	500 ml
⅓ cup	minced green onion	85 ml

1. In a small bowl whisk together mustard, vinegar, and lemon juice. Add garlic oil gradually, whisking constantly. Whisk in ¼ cup (60 ml) of the cheese. Season with salt and pepper. Cover and set aside for at least 1 hour or up to 1 day.

2. Bring a large pot of salted water to a boil over high heat; add florets and cook until tender-crisp. Drain and immediately plunge into ice water. When cool, drain again and pat dry. Broccoli may be cooked up to 6 hours ahead, cooled, and stored in the refrigerator.

3. Transfer broccoli to a large bowl along with tomatoes. Add dressing to vegetables and toss to coat well. Add green onion and remaining ¼ cup (60 ml) cheese and toss to blend. Taste and adjust seasoning before serving.

Serves 6.

Tricolor Salad

Flavorful oranges and grapefruits complement a hearty Herb and Garlic Vinaigrette. Watercress and endive lend their peppery and slightly bitter flavor to this composed salad studded with pomegranate seeds.

Herb and Garlic Vinaigrette

3 cloves	garlic, minced	3 cloves
1 tbl	Dijon mustard	1 tbl
1 tsp	salt	1 tsp
3 tbl	balsamic vinegar	3 tbl
7 tbl	extra virgin olive oil	7 tbl
1 tbl	parsley	1 tbl
1 tbl	chives	1 tbl
3–4 leaves	fresh basil	3–4 leaves
to taste	freshly ground black pepper	to taste
1	pomegranate	1
2	oranges	2
1	grapefruit	1
2 heads	Belgian endive	2 heads
2 bunches	watercress	2 bunches

1. To prepare Herb and Garlic Vinaigrette, whisk all ingredients together. Set aside and whisk again before serving.

2. Pull open pomegranate and reserve seeds. Peel and section oranges and grapefruit. Separate endive leaves. Arrange watercress in center of a 12- to 15-inch (30- to 37.5-cm) platter. Place endive leaves around perimeter like spokes in a wheel. Place a section of grapefruit and a section of orange between endive spokes.

3. Drizzle Herb and Garlic Vinaigrette over salad and dot with pomegranate seeds.

Serves 6.

DRAGON'S BREATH NOODLE SALAD

Asian flavors blended with the subtle texture of noodles create a satisfying main dish that garlic-loving vegetarians and meat-eaters alike will applaud, especially if you garnish it with Crisp Fried Garlic Chips (see page 94). The udon noodles in this recipe can be found in most natural food stores or Japanese markets. This dish tastes best when left to marinate for at least 45 minutes before serving, although it can be refrigerated for up to 48 hours. Add the peanuts at the last minute so they hold their crunch.

12 oz	Japanese udon noodles, cooked and drained	350 g
2 tbl	grated fresh ginger	2 tbl
5 oz	sliced water chestnuts	140 g
2 cups	sliced mushrooms	500 ml
2 tbl	Asian sesame oil	2 tbl
5 cloves	garlic, minced	5 cloves
6	green onions (including green part), minced	6
1–2 tsp	cayenne pepper	1–2 tsp
½ cup	soy sauce	125 ml
½ tsp	honey	½ tsp
½ cup	chopped peanuts	125 ml
as needed	lettuce leaves, for lining bowl	as needed
as needed	Crisp Fried Garlic Chips (see page 94), optional	as needed

1. Place pasta in a bowl. Mix together remaining ingredients except peanuts, lettuce, and Crisp Fried Garlic Chips, if used, and toss with pasta.

2. Let marinate for 45 minutes before serving. Add peanuts. Serve in a lettuce-lined bowl and sprinkle with Crisp Fried Garlic Chips, if desired.

Serves 4.

Pasta With Garlic, Fresh Tomatoes, and Basil

Delightfully simple and suffused with garlic, this dish works equally well as a first course or side dish.

1 lb	ripe tomatoes, peeled, seeded, and chopped	450 g
to taste	salt and freshly ground black pepper	to taste
2 cloves	garlic, minced	2 cloves
½ cup	extra virgin olive oil	125 ml
2 tbl	chopped fresh basil	2 tbl
½ lb	fettuccine, cooked and drained	225 g
3 tbl	extra virgin olive oil	3 tbl
to taste	salt and freshly ground black pepper	to taste
to taste	freshly grated Parmesan cheese	to taste

1. Mix tomatoes with salt, pepper, and garlic. Gradually stir in olive oil. Stir in basil. Let sauce stand at room temperature for 1–2 hours. Taste and add salt and pepper, if needed.

2. Place cooked pasta in a large serving bowl. Add olive oil and toss gently. Add mixture to pasta and toss again. Add salt, pepper, and cheese to taste. Serve immediately.

Serves 6.

The Many Faces of Garlic

Ivory cloves wrapped in an off-white husk characterize the most widely used variety of garlic, known as American or Californian. Other popular varieties include Society, Mexican White, Mexican Red, and Bavarian (or Rocombole), a top-setting variety. Mild-flavored elephant garlic (a relative of the smaller, more pungent varieties) develops heads weighing up to 1 pound (450 g) each. Next time you're at the farmer's market, acquaint yourself with some of the many faces of garlic.

GARLIC BUTTER

Spread this classic compound butter on bread or melt it onto meat, fish, or vegetables.

5 cloves	garlic, peeled	5 cloves
2 cups	water	500 ml
½ cup	butter, softened	125 ml

Boil garlic in water about 5 minutes. Drain, cool, then crush garlic and mix with butter.

Makes ½ cup (115 g).

GARLIC CROUTONS

Use these thin toasts for garnishing soups or as a foundation for creamy cheeses or spreads.

1	8-inch (20-cm) length of baguette	1
¼ cup	olive oil	60 ml
2 tbl	unsalted butter	2 tbl
1 clove	garlic, peeled and crushed	1 clove

Preheat oven to 350°F (175°C). Slice baguette on the diagonal about ¼ inch (.6 cm) thick. In a small saucepan over medium heat, heat olive oil, butter, and garlic until butter melts. Lightly brush both sides of bread with mixture and bake until golden brown (about 5 minutes).

Makes about 30 croutons.

GARLIC VINAIGRETTE

Vinaigrette is the classic French salad dressing. Made from blends of oil (usually olive or walnut) and wine vinegar, with minced garlic and other herbs added to taste, vinaigrettes are used to dress everything from simple lettuce salads to elaborate combinations of meats and vegetables. If you enjoy a strong garlic flavor, substitute ³/₄ cup (175 ml) garlic oil (see Making Garlic Oil on page 22) for the minced garlic and olive or walnut oil.

½ tbl	minced garlic	½ tbl
¾ cup	olive or walnut oil	175 ml
¼ cup	red wine vinegar	60 ml
to taste	salt and freshly ground black pepper	to taste

1. Cover ½ tablespoon minced garlic with ¾ cup (175 ml) olive oil and let stand overnight.

2. In a small bowl, combine vinegar, salt, and pepper. Whisk in the garlic-flavored oil and let stand 5 minutes. Whisk again, then taste and adjust seasoning.

Makes 1 cup (250 ml).

BAGNA CAUDA

This oil and garlic dip is a specialty of Italy's Piedmont region. The ingredients are few and simple, but they melt down into a rich bath for bread and vegetables that is addictive and highly aromatic.

½ cup	olive oil	125 ml
1 tbl	butter	1 tbl
½ tbl	minced garlic	½ tbl
2 oz	anchovy fillets, mashed	60 g
to taste	salt and freshly ground black pepper	to taste
as needed	cubes of day-old Italian bread	as needed
	whole artichokes, steamed and quartered, chokes removed	
	blanched cauliflower florets	
	raw fennel slices	
	raw carrot sticks	
	raw, sweet red-pepper strips	
	raw celery, pale inner stalks only	
	blanched asparagus spears	

1. In a small skillet over moderate heat, heat oil and butter until bubbly. Add garlic. Cook over low heat until fragrant; do not allow garlic to brown. Add anchovies and cook, stirring, for 2 minutes. Remove from heat; add salt and pepper to taste.

2. Transfer dip to a warm serving bowl or keep warm in a chafing dish. Serve with a platter of bread and assorted vegetables for dipping.

Serves 4.

SALSA VERDE

This famous Italian table sauce is nothing like the salsas used in Mexican cuisine. A garlic-tinged vinaigrette highlighted with the bright green tint of parsley and the fresh taste of garlic, Salsa Verde can be used to sauce roast lamb, grilled chicken wings, or broiled swordfish.

½ cup	olive oil	125 ml
2 tbl	red wine vinegar	2 tbl
1 tbl	capers	1 tbl
1 tsp	anchovy paste	1 tsp
1 bunch	parsley, finely chopped	1 bunch
1 clove	garlic, finely minced	1 clove

In a small bowl, stir together all ingredients.

Makes 1½ cups (350 ml).

BRAISED CHINESE CABBAGE AND GARLIC

Lily buds are the dried, unopened buds of a tiger lily. Soaked in water and drained, they add a pleasant texture and slightly tart, tealike flavor to this garlic-rich Chinese dish. Lily buds are available in Asian markets.

½ cup	dried lily buds	125 ml
as needed	peanut oil, for stir-frying	as needed
1 head	garlic, separated into cloves and peeled	1 head
1	carrot, peeled and sliced on the diagonal	1
1 tbl	minced fresh ginger	1 tbl
1 lb	Chinese cabbage, cut crosswise into 1½-inch (3.75-cm) slices	450 g
2–3	green onions, trimmed and cut into 2-inch (5-cm) lengths	2–3
1 cup	chicken stock, salted to taste	250 ml
1 tbl	soy sauce or tamari	1 tbl

1. In a small bowl soak lily buds in lukewarm water until soft. Drain, squeezing out excess liquid. Cut or pinch off hard ends, and set lily buds aside.

2. Have ready a 1½-quart (1.4-l) flameproof covered casserole. Heat a wok or skillet over medium heat. Add a tablespoon of oil, and stir-fry garlic cloves and carrot until lightly browned. Add ginger and stir-fry until fragrant. Transfer contents of wok to casserole. Add a little more oil to wok, and stir-fry cabbage and green onions until just heated through. Transfer to casserole. Add stock, soy sauce, and lily buds to wok and bring just to a boil. Pour over vegetables in casserole.

3. Place casserole over medium-low heat, bring to a simmer, and cover. Simmer 15–20 minutes. Serve directly from casserole.

Serves 4.

CABBAGES AND THE KING

From crunchy Thai salads to fiery Korean kimchee and Chinese Tientsin (pickled condiments), stuffings for wontons and spring rolls, fried rice, and a multitude of braised delicacies, cabbage and "the king of herbs" are a favorite combination in Asian cuisines. The flavor and aroma of garlic, whether simmered, sautéed, deep-fried, baked, grilled, or uncooked, finds an ideal companion in the earthy succulence of cabbage—both Dutch and other round-headed Western varieties as well as napa, bok choy, and similar Asian varieties with looser, more elongated leaves.

PEPERONATA

Sweet peppers stewed with tomatoes, herbs, and garlic are a popular antipasto in southern Italy. Serve with crusty bread to mop up the aromatic juices. Select firm peppers that feel heavy for their size.

½ cup	olive oil	125 ml
2 tbl	minced garlic	2 tbl
½	yellow onion, minced	½
2	red bell peppers	2
2	green bell peppers	2
1	yellow bell pepper	1
2	tomatoes, peeled, seeded, and coarsely chopped	2
2 tsp	salt	2 tsp
¼ cup	fresh oregano leaves	60 ml
½	red onion, thinly sliced, for garnish	½
2 tbl	minced parsley, for garnish	2 tbl
2 tbl	fruity extra virgin olive oil (optional)	2 tbl

1. In a large skillet over medium heat, heat the ½ cup (125 ml) olive oil until it is hot but not smoking. Add garlic and onion and sauté, stirring until lightly colored (about 3 minutes).

2. Halve peppers; remove seeds and trim away white ribs. Cut lengthwise into strips ½ inch (1.25 cm) wide. Add all peppers to skillet at one time and stir to blend with garlic-onion mixture. Add tomatoes and salt and mix gently. Scatter oregano leaves across top. Cover and simmer slowly until peppers are soft (12–15 minutes). Remove from heat and transfer to serving bowl to cool.

3. Serve peppers at room temperature, garnishing with the sliced red onion and minced parsley. If desired, drizzle with the 2 tablespoons fruity olive oil just before serving.

Serves 4.

MIXED GRILL WITH GARLIC RUB

Summer vegetables benefit from a rubdown with garlic before grilling. Serve the Mixed Grill with freshly made Aioli (see page 38).

1 (about 1 lb)	eggplant	1 (about 450 g)
1 lb	zucchini	450 g
1 lb	yellow pattypan squash	450 g
2	red bell peppers	2
1 bunch	green onions	1 bunch
½ cup	olive oil	125 ml
2 tbl	minced garlic	2 tbl
to taste	salt and freshly ground black pepper	to taste
1	lemon (optional)	1
1 recipe	Aioli (see page 38)	1 recipe

1. Wash vegetables and pat dry, leaving stems on eggplant, zucchini, and pattypan squash. Cut eggplant and zucchini lengthwise into 1-inch (2.5-cm) slices. Quarter pattypan squash. Stem, seed, and cut peppers into quarters. Remove roots from green onions.

2. On a baking sheet mix oil, garlic, salt, and pepper. Rub surfaces of vegetables with oil mixture. Be sure all surfaces of eggplant and squashes are well coated.

3. Prepare fire for direct-heat method of cooking (place food directly above heat source). When fire is ready, place vegetables on preheated grill or grill pan. Quick hands and a pair of tongs are important because the oil coating will cause flare-ups; close the lid as soon as possible.

4. After 5–6 minutes, flip vegetables over with a spatula, arranging vegetables on grill so they don't fall into the briquettes. Vegetables should be done in another 5–6 minutes. Squeeze lemon over vegetables as they finish cooking, if desired. Serve with Aioli.

Serves 4.

Tuscan-Style Roasted Potatoes

These crusty baked potato wedges get the classic Tuscan treatment: a basting of olive oil and a dusting of garlic and Parmesan cheese.

3	baking potatoes	3
¾ cup (approx.)	olive oil	175 ml (approx.)
to taste	salt	to taste
1 tbl	minced garlic	1 tbl
2 tbl	freshly grated Parmesan cheese	2 tbl

1. Preheat oven to 375°F (190°C). Wash potatoes, dry well, and quarter lengthwise. Coat a heavy baking sheet with oil; arrange potatoes on sheet. Rub them well all over with olive oil, then dust with salt. Bake, basting every 10 minutes with oil, until well browned and cooked through (30–45 minutes).

2. When potatoes are almost tender, heat ¼ cup (60 ml) olive oil in a small saucepan or skillet over moderately low heat. Add garlic and cook 1 minute, stirring constantly. Strain, setting garlic aside and reserving oil for another use.

3. Transfer potatoes to a warm serving platter; sprinkle with garlic and cheese. Serve immediately.

Serves 4.

SWEET POTATO SAUTÉ

Rich in vitamin A, sweet potatoes are wonderful prepared with garlic and cream to enhance their earthy flavor.

4	sweet potatoes, peeled	4
4 tbl	butter	4 tbl
1	onion, minced	1
3 cloves	garlic, minced	3 cloves
1½ tsp	salt	1½ tsp
¼ tsp	freshly ground black pepper	¼ tsp
5 tbl	whipping cream	5 tbl

1. Cut potatoes into fine julienne strips about ⅛ inch (.3 cm) thick by 2 inches (5 cm) long. In a 14-inch (35-cm) skillet over medium heat, melt butter and sauté onion and garlic. Add julienned sweet potatoes and cook for 10 minutes, stirring constantly.

2. Stir in salt, pepper, and cream, and cook for 5 minutes more. Serve immediately.

Serves 6.

COOKING WITH PARCHMENT

Parchment paper, available in most supermarkets and specialty food shops, is a great tool for keeping baked foods moist and tender while cooking. Cooking food in parchment paper—en papillote—also helps retain flavor by sealing in natural juices and seasonings. Parchment cooking works best with fish, poultry, and vegetables, so experiment with herbs—including garlic—spices, lemon juice, and wine to create a moist, flavorful dish. Clean-up is easy: Simply discard the parchment paper after the food has been served.

POTATOES, SHALLOTS, AND GARLIC EN PAPILLOTE

The ingredients in the compound butter that flavors these potato packets are few and simple, but the results are delightful. The packets can be readied early in the day and baked just before dinnertime. At serving time, use caution in opening the steam-filled packets.

Rosemary-Garlic Butter

¾ cup	unsalted butter, softened	175 ml
3 cloves	garlic, minced	3 cloves
3 tbl	fresh rosemary, minced	3 tbl
1½ tbl	freshly squeezed lemon juice	1½ tbl
¾ tsp	salt	¾ tsp
½ tsp	freshly ground white pepper	½ tsp
16 (about 2 lb)	red potatoes	16 (about 900 g)
16	shallots, peeled	16
16 cloves	garlic, peeled	16 cloves
2 tsp	salt	2 tsp
1 tsp	freshly ground black pepper	1 tsp

1. To prepare Rosemary-Garlic Butter, in a small bowl stir together all ingredients. Set aside.

2. Preheat oven to 350°F (175°C). Slice potatoes ¼ inch (.6 cm) thick. On each of eight 8-inch (20-cm) squares of parchment paper or aluminum foil, place 2 sliced potatoes, 2 shallots, and 2 cloves garlic. Dot each serving with 1½ tablespoons Rosemary-Garlic Butter, and add 1 tablespoon of water, ¼ teaspoon salt, and ⅛ teaspoon pepper. Seal packets tightly.

3. Place packets on a baking sheet; bake 40 minutes. Remove from oven, carefully open packets, and slide potatoes, shallots, and garlic onto plates. Serve at once.

Serves 8.

MAIN EVENTS

The perfect foil for meats, seafood, poultry, and pasta, garlic can turn a tasty main dish into a pungent, powerful pièce de résistance. Whether they be treasured favorites or contemporary variations on classics, the following recipes have one thing in common: All are infused with the magical powers of garlic.

BASIL-STUFFED BREASTS OF CHICKEN

If you've never before tried placing stuffing under the skin of poultry, these chicken breasts inspired by the cuisine of Provence practically guarantee success. Use extra virgin olive oil, fresh basil, and tender young garlic cloves for the best flavor.

1 cup	dry bread crumbs	250 ml
2 tbl	chopped fresh basil	2 tbl
2 cloves	garlic, minced	2 cloves
as needed	extra virgin olive oil	as needed
2	whole chicken breasts, boned and halved	2
to taste	salt	to taste

1. Preheat oven to 350°F (175°C). In a medium bowl combine bread crumbs and basil. Add garlic and 1 tablespoon of the olive oil, mixing with fingers to moisten crumbs. Set aside.

2. Wash chicken breasts and pat dry. Sprinkle with salt. Lay each breast, skin side up, on a cutting board. Loosen the skin from the breasts by gently sliding the fingertips between the skin and the breast meat.

3. Insert ¼ cup (60 ml) stuffing under the skin of each breast, centering the stuffing in the middle of the breast. Fold skin and meat under to form a dome and tie the breast with kitchen string. Brush with additional olive oil.

4. Place the prepared breasts skin side up in a shallow, oiled baking dish. Bake on middle rack of oven 35 minutes.

5. When breasts are done, cool slightly, remove string, and serve.

Serves 4.

STIR-FRIED CHICKEN WITH THAI BASIL AND GARLIC

In Southeast Asian cooking, fresh Thai basil is used not only as a seasoning herb but also sautéed as a leafy vegetable. Five cloves of garlic intensify the flavor of this fiery dish. The fish sauce, oyster sauce, and Thai basil are available in Asian markets.

2 tbl	peanut or corn oil	2 tbl
5 cloves	garlic, chopped	5 cloves
1 lb	chicken meat, preferably dark, cut into 1-inch by ½-inch (2.5-cm by 1.25-cm) pieces	450 g
6	serrano chiles, seeded and cut in half lengthwise	6
3	green onions, cut into 2-inch (5-cm) lengths	3
1 tsp	sugar	1 tsp
1 tbl	Thai fish sauce	1 tbl
2 tsp	oyster sauce	2 tsp
2 tbl	chicken stock	2 tbl
1 cup	fresh Thai basil leaves	250 ml
as needed	cooked white long-grain rice, for accompaniment	as needed

1. Preheat wok over medium-high heat until hot, then pour in oil. Add garlic and cook until lightly browned (about 45 seconds). Add chicken in batches and stir-fry until it feels firm to the touch (about 1 minute). Add chiles, green onions, sugar, fish sauce, oyster sauce, and stock; stir-fry until sauce thickens (about 45 seconds).

2. Add basil and cook just until leaves are wilted (about 10 seconds). Serve hot over rice.

Serves 4 with other dishes.

MEDITERRANEAN CHICKEN

Mediterranean Chicken delights with its unusual flavor combination of garlic, herbs, Greek olives, and heady balsamic vinegar. If possible, let the chicken marinate for several hours, basting frequently with the sauce, and then roast it right before serving. It is also delicious served cold for supper the next day, with a glass of white wine and a green salad.

as needed	oil, for coating pan	as needed
one (3 lb)	roasting chicken	one (1.4 kg)
2 cloves	garlic	2 cloves
2 tbl	green olive oil	2 tbl
1 tbl	minced fresh tarragon	1 tbl
1 tsp	crushed sage	1 tsp
6 tbl	balsamic vinegar	6 tbl
6	new potatoes	6
¼ cup	pitted Greek olives	60 ml

1. Preheat oven to 375°F (190°C). Lightly oil a large roasting pan or deep casserole.

2. Remove skin from chicken, if desired. Place chicken in roasting pan, breast side up. Peel and halve garlic cloves, rub surface of chicken with cut garlic, then place cloves inside chicken.

3. Mix together olive oil, tarragon, sage, and vinegar. Pour over surface of chicken and inside cavity. Cut potatoes in quarters and place olives and potatoes around chicken. Cover pan and place in oven.

4. Roast until juice runs clear when a sharp knife is inserted into thigh of bird (45 minutes–1 hour). Slice or cut into serving pieces and serve with olives, potatoes, and cooking liquid.

Serves 6.

CHICKEN ALI BABA

The 40 cloves of garlic sweeten and soften as they roast with the chicken. For a wonderful sauce, purée the cooked cloves and combine with the poultry juices. Note that the chicken must marinate for 30 minutes before roasting.

1	lemon	1
one (3–4 lb)	roasting chicken	one (1.4–1.8 kg)
1 tsp	salt	1 tsp
½ tsp	freshly ground black pepper	½ tsp
40 cloves (3 heads)	garlic	40 cloves (3 heads)
4 tbl	unsalted butter	4 tbl
2 tbl	olive oil	2 tbl
1 cup	chicken stock	250 ml
1 bunch	parsley, minced, for garnish	1 bunch

1. Preheat oven to 375°F (190°C). Cut lemon in half and squeeze juice over chicken. Sprinkle salt and pepper over chicken and rub in. Marinate 30 minutes.

2. Remove papery husk from garlic heads. Separate cloves from heads but do not peel. In a 4- to 5-quart (3.6- to 4.5-l) Dutch oven or heatproof casserole, brown chicken (breast side down) in butter and oil over medium heat (about 5 minutes). Add garlic cloves and stock to pan. Stir to coat with oil. Cover and roast in oven 60–70 minutes.

3. Remove chicken to serving platter. Degrease pan juices. Purée garlic cloves and remaining pan juices through a food mill or sieve. Pour purée over chicken and sprinkle with parsley.

Serves 6.

GARLIC WINGS

Bake, broil, or grill these chicken wings. Baking instructions are given below; you can broil these wings in only 5 to 6 minutes. Perhaps the tastiest results come from the charcoal grill, which requires 12 to 15 minutes basting and grilling time.

½ cup	dry sherry	125 ml
2 tbl each	sherry vinegar and lemon juice	2 tbl each
1 tbl each	tomato paste and sugar	1 tbl each
2 tbl	minced garlic	2 tbl
2 tsp	salt	2 tsp
2 tbl	ground cumin	2 tbl
½ tsp	cayenne pepper	½ tsp
24	chicken drummettes (see below)	24
2 tbl	chopped cilantro (coriander leaves), for garnish	2 tbl

1. In a glass bowl, combine sherry, vinegar, lemon juice, tomato paste, sugar, garlic, salt, cumin, and cayenne. Marinate chicken in mixture for at least 4 hours or overnight.

2. Preheat oven to 350°F (175°C). Bake uncovered for 45 minutes. Serve hot, garnished with chopped cilantro.

Makes 24 drummettes.

WING IT

Many markets sell what looks like tiny chicken legs, called "drummettes." These are not legs from miniature chickens, but wings with the tips removed—something you can do yourself if you prefer. They have great charm: They can be marinated ahead of time, and, because they are so small, they are perfect finger food—easy to pick up and hold, and gone in a bite or two. In fact, chicken wings are so appealing you might want to prepare an extra batch; they disappear like popcorn.

SHRIMP WITH GARLIC AND CHIVES

Fresh garlic is the most popular flavoring for sautéed shrimp. The chives add color and extra zest. Serve these buttery shrimp with rice and a green vegetable, such as broccoli, green beans, or snow peas.

1½ lb	raw shrimp, shelled and deveined	680 g
1 tbl	olive oil	1 tbl
¼ cup	butter	60 ml
to taste	salt and freshly ground black pepper	to taste
1	shallot, finely chopped	1
3 cloves	garlic, minced	3 cloves
2 tbl	finely sliced chives	2 tbl

1. Pat shrimp thoroughly dry with paper towels.

2. Heat oil and 3 tablespoons of the butter in a large frying pan over medium-high heat. Add half the shrimp and sprinkle with salt and pepper. Sauté, tossing often, until shrimp are pink (about 1½ minutes). Transfer to a platter, using a slotted spoon. Repeat with remaining shrimp.

3. Add remaining 1 tablespoon butter to pan. Reduce heat to low. Stir in shallot and garlic and cook a few seconds. Return shrimp to pan and add any juices that collected in platter. Cook, tossing often, for 1 minute. Add chives and toss over low heat for a few seconds.

4. Transfer shrimp to platter, spoon the juices from the pan over them, and serve.

Serves 4.

POLYNESIAN PRAWNS WITH PLUM SAUCE

A zesty sweet-and-sour plum sauce redolent with garlic is the partner for these prawns. Serve with chilled beer—or Mai Tais for an island flavor. Be sure to serve prawns with cocktail picks and plenty of napkins.

3 lb	prawns, boiled and shelled	1.4 kg
2 tbl	minced parsley	2 tbl
1 tsp	grated lemon zest	1 tsp

Plum Sauce

4 tsp	cornstarch	4 tsp
1 cup	water	250 ml
⅔ cup	plum preserves	150 ml
½ cup	apricot-pineapple preserves	125 ml
6 tbl	rice vinegar	6 tbl
4 cloves	garlic, minced	4 cloves
2 tsp	minced ginger	2 tsp
1 tsp	salt	1 tsp
1 tsp	hot-pepper flakes	1 tsp

1. Arrange prawns on a serving platter. Combine parsley and lemon zest and sprinkle over prawns.

2. To prepare Plum Sauce, in a small saucepan dissolve cornstarch in the water. Add preserves and vinegar. Place garlic and ginger on cutting board; sprinkle with salt, and mash repeatedly with the side of a wide-bladed knife to make a rough paste. Add paste and hot-pepper flakes to sauce. Bring sauce to a boil and reduce to a simmer. Cook until slightly thickened.

3. Serve sauce at room temperature with prawns.

Serves 10.

HANGTOWN FRY CANTONESE

Present this stir-fry of oysters and garlic-flavored eggs on slices of toasted French baguette, spoon it over rice, or fill a baked pastry shell with it. Serve as a first course or a light luncheon dish.

4 tbl	peanut oil	4 tbl
1 slice	fresh ginger, bruised	1 slice
as needed	flour, for coating	as needed
1 lb	shucked oysters, drained	450 g
to taste	salt and white pepper	to taste
½	onion, cut lengthwise into ¼-inch (.6-cm) strips	½
2 cloves	garlic, finely minced	2 cloves
1 cup	chopped chives, preferably Chinese garlic chives	250 ml
5	eggs, slightly beaten	5
1 tbl	oyster sauce, for drizzling (optional)	1 tbl

1. Preheat wok over medium-high heat until hot, then pour in 2 tablespoons of the oil. Add ginger. Meanwhile, lightly flour oysters. When oil is fragrant, add floured oysters and fry until golden brown (about 1 minute per side). Add salt and pepper. Remove to a plate and keep warm.

2. Rinse wok with hot water and wipe dry with a paper towel. Preheat wok over high heat until hot; then pour in remaining 2 tablespoons oil. When hot add onion and stir-fry 15 seconds. Add garlic and chives; toss until chives begin to wilt (about 10 seconds). Add eggs and toss gently (do not stir) with greens until eggs are loosely scrambled; cook until set but not dry (about 1 minute). Fold in reserved oysters. Transfer to a serving platter and drizzle with oyster sauce, if used.

Serves 6.

SEAFOOD WITH KIWI

In this eye-catching entrée, the sweet taste of kiwifruit, the tartness of lemon, and the bite of garlic offer a tantalizing contrast to the delicate seafood. If the shrimp are large enough to have grit in the intestinal vein, devein them before cooking. Fillets of any white-fleshed fish can be substituted for the shrimp and halibut, and slices of nectarine, papaya, orange, or grapefruit can replace the kiwi.

2 tbl each	butter and olive oil	2 tbl each
3 cloves	garlic, minced or pressed	3 cloves
¾ lb	medium shrimp, peeled, tails intact	350 g
¾ lb	halibut, cut in 1-inch (2.5-cm) pieces	350 g
2	kiwifruit, peeled and sliced	2
¼ cup	lemon juice	60 ml
¼ cup	minced fresh parsley	60 ml
1	lemon wheel, sliced in half, for garnish (optional)	1

1. In a large frying pan over medium heat, melt butter with oil. Add garlic, shrimp, and halibut; sauté just until shrimp begin to turn pink and halibut becomes opaque (4 minutes).

2. Push seafood to edges of pan and warm kiwi briefly in center.

3. Combine lemon juice and parsley and gently mix with seafood mixture.

4. Garnish with lemon wheel, if desired, and serve at once.

Serves 4.

INDONESIAN CRAB CURRY

Serve this garlicky Southeast Asian specialty with small garnishes of chopped dried fruits, cilantro, and lime slices. You can buy shrimp paste and Thai fish sauce in most Asian markets.

1½ tsp	cayenne pepper	1½ tsp
1 tsp	grated fresh ginger	1 tsp
½ tsp	freshly ground black pepper	½ tsp
4 cloves	garlic, minced	4 cloves
5	shallots, minced	5
⅓ cup	chopped fresh coriander (including stems, leaves, and roots)	85 ml
½ tsp	grated lime zest	½ tsp
½ tsp	salt	½ tsp
1 tsp	dried shrimp paste (optional)	1 tsp
½ cup	grated coconut	125 ml
2 cups	milk	500 ml
2 tbl	Thai fish sauce or soy sauce	2 tbl
1 tbl	honey	1 tbl
1 lb	cooked crabmeat	450 g
5 cups	cooked brown rice	1.1 l

1. In a stockpot combine cayenne, ginger, pepper, garlic, shallots, coriander, lime zest, salt, shrimp paste (if used), coconut, and milk. Bring to a boil and cook over medium-high heat for 10 minutes.

2. Add fish sauce, honey, and crabmeat. Heat through. Serve hot over rice.

Serves 6.

Roasted Salmon With Garlic Cream

Simmering whole garlic cloves renders them soft and mild. Purée the softened cloves with butter and cream, spread it on the salmon, and bake until done to your liking. This dish couldn't be simpler or more aromatic. Note that the salmon should marinate for at least 30 minutes before baking.

4 heads	garlic	4 heads
3 tbl	butter	3 tbl
1 cup	sour cream	250 ml
1 tsp	stone-ground mustard	1 tsp
4 (about 2 lb)	fresh salmon fillets	4 (about 900 g)

1. Remove papery outer husk from garlic, but leave heads intact and cloves unpeeled. Place heads in a saucepan just large enough to hold them. Add water to barely cover and bring to a simmer over high heat. Reduce heat to maintain a simmer and cook 40 minutes, adding more water as necessary to keep heads barely covered. Remove from heat, cool, and peel. Cloves will be very soft and easy to peel. Place cloves in a food processor with butter and purée. Add sour cream and mustard and process until blended. Transfer to a bowl and set aside.

2. Place salmon in glass dish. Spread top surface of each fillet with some of the garlic purée. Cover with plastic wrap and refrigerate for at least 30 minutes or up to 1 day.

3. Preheat oven to 350°F (175°C). Place fillets on a lightly buttered baking sheet or in a buttered baking dish and roast until done to taste (7–10 minutes). Serve immediately.

Serves 4.

ROCKFISH VERACRUZ

This dish can also be made with 1 pound (450 g) of rockfish and 1 pound (450 g) of prawns. The garlic and chile flavors go well with hot buttered corn tortillas.

½ cup	flour	125 ml
2 tsp	salt	2 tsp
1 tsp	freshly ground black pepper	1 tsp
2 lb	rockfish fillets	900 g
¾ cup	clarified butter	175 ml
4–6 cloves	garlic, thinly sliced	4–6 cloves
¼ cup	olive oil	60 ml
2	onions, sliced in ¼-inch (.6-cm) rings	2
2	bell peppers, sliced in ¼-inch (.6-cm) rings	2
4	tomatoes, peeled, seeded, and chopped	4
2–3	jalapeño chiles, seeded and cut in thin strips	2–3
1	avocado, peeled, halved, and sliced in ¼-inch (.6-cm) segments	1

1. Combine flour, 1 teaspoon of the salt, and ½ teaspoon of the pepper. Pat fillets dry, then dust with seasoned flour.

2. In large sauté pan over low heat, melt butter. Add garlic; sauté 1 minute. Add fillets and sauté on each side until golden.

3. Arrange fish on large, warm serving platter.

4. In another pan heat olive oil. Add onions and cook until they begin to wilt. Add bell peppers, tomatoes, jalapeño chiles, remaining 1 teaspoon salt, and remaining ½ teaspoon pepper. Stir and cook, uncovered, for 5 minutes. Cover and simmer 10 minutes. Correct seasonings.

5. Pour sauce over fillets. Arrange avocado slices around fish.

Serves 6.

MARINATED BEEF-GARLIC KABOBS

Lean chunks of beef are marinated in a tenderizing sauce of ginger, yogurt, and curry, and skewered alternately with slices of garlic before being grilled. You can marinate the beef overnight, in a tightly covered container, and grill right before serving. Serve kabobs with a marinated tomato salad or coleslaw.

2 lb	lean beef, cubed	900 g
2 tbl	grated fresh ginger	2 tbl
2 tsp	salt	2 tsp
1 tsp	hot chile oil	1 tsp
2 tsp	curry powder	2 tsp
1 cup	plain yogurt	250 ml
8 cloves	garlic, peeled and sliced	8 cloves
4 cups	cooked brown rice (optional)	900 ml

1. Trim fat off beef cubes and place beef in a shallow bowl.

2. Mix ginger, salt, oil, curry, and yogurt. Pour over beef. Let beef marinate for 24 hours. Stir occasionally.

3. Soak 12 bamboo skewers in salted water for 20 minutes.

4. Preheat broiler. Skewer beef cubes alternately with slices of garlic, pressing both together as tightly as possible on the skewers.

5. Broil kabobs for 5 minutes, turning to brown all sides. Serve over rice, if desired.

Serves 6.

BRAISED BEEF WITH MUSHROOMS

Garlic and herbs flavor this French stew (see photo on page 10).

3 lb	lean beef, cut in 1-inch (2.5-cm) cubes	1.4 kg
1¾ cups	dry red wine	425 ml
5 tbl	olive oil	5 tbl
2	onions, thinly slivered	2
2 cloves	garlic, minced	2 cloves
1 tsp	salt	1 tsp
½ tsp each	sugar, peppercorns, juniper berries, and dried thyme	½ tsp each
⅛ tsp each	whole cloves and ground nutmeg	⅛ tsp each
1	bay leaf	1
½ lb	mushrooms, quartered	225 g
1 cup	canned beef stock	250 ml
1 tbl	tomato paste	1 tbl
1 tbl	cornstarch, blended with 2 tbl beef stock	1 tbl
as needed	chopped parsley, for garnish	as needed

1. Mix beef in a bowl with wine and 1 tablespoon of the oil. Add onions, garlic, salt, sugar, peppercorns, juniper berries, thyme, cloves, nutmeg, and bay leaf. Cover and refrigerate overnight. Strain and reserve marinade; pat beef dry.

2. In a large pan, heat remaining oil over medium heat. Add mushrooms; cook until browned; remove. In same pan brown beef. Add onions; cook until limp. Return mushrooms to pan. Add stock, tomato paste, and marinade. Bring to a boil, cover, then simmer until tender (2½ hours).

3. Drain cooking liquid and skim fat. Boil until reduced by about a fourth. Remove from heat and blend in cornstarch mixture. Cook, stirring often, until thickened and clear. Pour sauce over beef and mushrooms. Garnish with parsley.

Serves 6.

CHILI AJO

Garlic and beer enliven this beef-lover's chili.

⅓ cup (approx.)	olive oil	85 ml (approx.)
6 lb	beef chuck, cubed	2.8 kg
4 cups	minced onion	900 ml
⅓ cup	minced garlic	85 ml
3 cups (approx.)	beef stock	700 ml (approx.)
3 cups	flat beer	700 ml
1½ cups	water	350 ml
¼ cup	chili powder	60 ml
6 cans (15 oz each)	tomatoes, drained and chopped	6 cans (450 ml each)
⅓ cup	tomato paste	85 ml
1½ tbl	minced fresh oregano	1½ tbl
3 tbl	cumin seed	3 tbl
to taste	salt	to taste
to taste	cayenne pepper	to taste
as needed	cornmeal	as needed

1. In a skillet over moderately high heat, warm 3 tablespoons of the oil. Brown beef in batches, adding more oil as necessary. Transfer meat to a large stockpot when well browned.

2. Reduce heat to low. Add onion and garlic and sauté until soft (about 10 minutes). Place in stockpot along with stock, beer, water, chili powder, tomatoes, tomato paste, and oregano.

3. In a small skillet over low heat, toast cumin seed until fragrant. Grind in a blender. Add to stockpot.

4. Add salt and cayenne to taste. Simmer, partially covered, until beef is tender (about 1½ hours). Add more stock if mixture is dry. If chili is thin, stir in up to 2 tablespoons cornmeal and cook 5 minutes longer.

Serves 12.

TANDOORI BUTTERFLY

Butterflied leg of lamb, flavored and moistened with a spicy, garlicky marinade, is an ideal cut for broiling or rapid grilling on a barbecue.

½ tsp	cumin seed, toasted and ground	½ tsp
1	lime, juiced	1
1 cup	plain yogurt	250 ml
1 tbl	grated fresh ginger	1 tbl
1 tbl	minced cilantro (coriander leaves)	1 tbl
½ tsp	ground anise or fennel seed	½ tsp
¼ tsp	ground mustard	¼ tsp
1 tbl	cayenne pepper, or to taste	1 tbl
1 tbl	paprika	1 tbl
2 tbl	minced garlic	2 tbl
½ tsp	salt	½ tsp
1 (about 4 lb)	butterflied whole leg of lamb	1 (about 1.8 kg)

1. To prepare marinade, in a bowl mix all ingredients except lamb.

2. Steep lamb in marinade for at least 2 hours at room temperature or, preferably, overnight in refrigerator. Bring meat to room temperature; remove meat from marinade, reserving marinade.

3. Preheat broiler or, if using an outdoor grill, allow coals in grill to burn down to white ash. Place lamb about 3 inches (7.5 cm) from heat source and broil 8–10 minutes per side for medium-rare, basting every few minutes with reserved marinade.

Serves 8.

LAMBCAKES IN HERB SAUCE

Accompany these garlic-laden lamb burgers with a salad for a light but satisfying supper.

as needed	salt	as needed
1 lb	ground lamb	450 g
2 tbl	cracked black peppercorns	2 tbl
2 cups	water	500 ml
1 head	garlic	1 head
1	tomato, peeled, seeded, and minced	1
½ cup	finely chopped fresh basil, mint, or parsley	125 ml
1 tbl	butter, cut into 4 pieces	1 tbl

1. Mix ½ teaspoon salt with lamb, shape meat into 4 patties, and coat both sides of patties with peppercorns, pushing peppercorns into meat with the heel of the hand. Let stand at room temperature for 1 hour.

2. Meanwhile bring the water to a boil. Separate garlic head into cloves. Drop cloves into boiling water; lower heat and simmer until garlic is very tender and mild (about 25 minutes). Drain garlic and peel, reserving water.

3. Heat a heavy nonstick medium skillet until waves of heat ripple up from surface. Sear lamb patties in dry skillet for 2 minutes per side. Transfer to warmed platter. Add to skillet the poached garlic, ¼ cup (60 ml) water from the garlic, tomato, and basil. Reduce sauce rapidly to a glaze, stirring constantly. With pan off heat, whisk butter, a piece at a time, into warm sauce. Season with salt to taste and pour sauce over lamb.

Serves 4.

PASTA WITH GARLIC-PARMESAN CREAM

What makes this simple dish from northern Italy truly special is the delicate sauce, lightly laced with garlic, which you can use to dress up almost any pasta, fresh or dried. Bathe fettuccine in it and you'll have something very much like classic Fettuccine Alfredo. The sauce can be made up to four hours ahead and refrigerated. Reheat gently before serving over freshly cooked pasta.

2 tbl	olive oil	2 tbl
1 tbl	butter	1 tbl
2 tbl	finely minced garlic	2 tbl
1 cup	heavy cream	250 ml
¾ cup	freshly grated Parmesan cheese	175 ml
to taste	freshly ground white or black pepper	to taste
12 oz	fresh pasta	350 g
2 tbl	chopped parsley, for garnish	2 tbl

1. Heat olive oil and butter in a skillet over moderate heat. Add garlic; cook gently until soft but do not allow to brown.

2. Add cream; cook over low heat 3–4 minutes more, whisking to incorporate cream. Stir in ½ cup (125 ml) of the cheese and white or black pepper to taste. Remove from heat and set aside.

3. Cook and drain fresh pasta. Add garlic-Parmesan cream mixture and toss gently. Sprinkle remaining cheese over pasta and garnish with parsley. Serve at once.

Serves 4.

Pizza With Pesto and Fontina

A hint of garlic enhances the robust flavor of the pesto topping on this mouthwatering meatless pizza.

Pesto

2 cups	lightly packed fresh basil leaves	500 ml
¼ cup	olive oil	60 ml
1 tsp	lemon juice	1 tsp
1 clove	garlic, minced or pressed	1 clove
2 tbl	pine nuts (optional)	2 tbl
⅔ cup	freshly grated Parmesan cheese	150 ml
2 tbl	olive oil	2 tbl
½ lb	mushrooms, thinly sliced	225 g
3 cups	grated Fontina cheese	700 ml
1	14-inch (35-cm) unbaked pizza crust	1

1. To make pesto, rinse basil leaves well and pat dry before measuring. In blender combine basil, oil, lemon juice, garlic, pine nuts (if used), and Parmesan cheese. Purée and set aside.

2. Preheat oven to 450°F (230°C). Heat the oil in a frying pan over medium-high heat. Add mushrooms and cook, stirring, until mushrooms are lightly browned and their liquid has cooked away. Remove from heat.

3. Sprinkle Fontina cheese over the pizza. Arrange mushrooms over cheese; drizzle with remaining oil.

4. Bake on lowest rack of oven until crust browns (about 25 minutes). Spoon pesto evenly over pizza. Return to oven long enough to heat pesto through (1–2 minutes). Cut into wedges and serve at once.

Makes one 14-inch (35-cm) pizza.

CHICAGO-STYLE DEEP-DISH PIZZA

This garlic-enhanced version of a traditional favorite unites Italian sausage, cheese, mushrooms, and tomato sauce. Try adding a handful of chopped Sunless Dried Tomatoes With Garlic (see page 16) to the bottled pizza sauce, and feel free to substitute your own favorite toppings, from anchovies to zucchini.

¾ lb	Italian sausage	350 g
2 cloves	garlic, minced	2 cloves
as needed	olive oil	as needed
1	16-inch (40-cm) unbaked pizza crust	1
4 cups	grated mozzarella cheese	900 ml
½ lb	mushrooms, thinly sliced	225 g
1½ cups	bottled pizza sauce	350 ml
⅓ cup	freshly grated Parmesan cheese	85 ml

1. Preheat oven to 450°F (230°C). Crumble sausage meat into a large frying pan over medium-high heat. Add garlic and cook, stirring often, until lightly browned. Pour off drippings and discard. Set sausage aside.

2. Oil a 15-inch (37.5-cm) deep-dish pizza pan and line with pizza crust, pressing dough up sides of pan.

3. Sprinkle half of the mozzarella over the dough. Cover with an even layer of mushrooms, then with cooked sausage. Spread the sauce over sausage. Cover with remaining mozzarella and top with the Parmesan cheese.

4. Bake on lowest rack of oven until crust browns well (20–25 minutes). Serve at once.

Makes one 15-inch (37.5-cm) deep-dish pizza.

Encore: Garlic Takes a Final Bow

For a meal to remember, don't let the curtain close until you've served this showstopper: Stinking Rose Ice Cream (see recipe on opposite page), perhaps topped with Crisp Fried Garlic Chips (see page 94). A perfect tribute to the illustrious bulb, this deceptively delicious dessert will receive a standing ovation from garlic lovers everywhere.

STINKING ROSE ICE CREAM

If you enjoy avant-garde flavors of ice cream, you'll have to try this one to believe it. Use more or less garlic, according to your tolerance. Confirmed "garlic heads" will want to add a sprinkling of Crisp Fried Garlic Chips (see page 94). This ice cream is best when served soon after it has been made, since the garlic flavor intensifies during storage in the freezer.

1½ cups	whipping cream	350 ml
½ cup	milk	125 ml
⅓ cup	sugar	85 ml
1 clove	garlic, crushed	1 clove
pinch	salt	pinch
2	egg yolks	2
1 tbl	honey	1 tbl
1 tsp	lemon juice	1 tsp

1. In a heavy-bottomed saucepan heat cream, milk, sugar, garlic, and salt, stirring occasionally, until sugar is melted and mixture is hot but not boiling.

2. Whisk egg yolks together in a bowl. Keep whisking and very slowly pour in 1 cup (250 ml) of the cream mixture. When smooth, pour back into pan of hot liquid. Cook, whisking constantly, until mixture thickens slightly and coats the back of a spoon (about 5 minutes). Be careful not to let mixture boil, or it will curdle. Strain into a clean bowl. Add honey and lemon juice, mixing well. Cool thoroughly.

3. Transfer to an ice cream machine and freeze according to manufacturer's instructions.

Makes about 1½ pints (750 ml).

CRISP FRIED GARLIC CHIPS

Southeast Asian dishes often call for fried garlic chips to garnish soups, noodles, and salads. It may be difficult to imagine, but they also are delicious with sweet dishes. To ensure even cooking, the garlic must be uniformly sliced. If the slices are fried until completely dry, they will keep several weeks in an airtight tin.

12 cloves	garlic	12 cloves
2 cups	peanut oil	500 ml
to taste	salt	to taste

1. Peel garlic and cut crosswise into slices that are uniformly paper-thin.

2. Preheat wok over medium heat until hot. Pour in oil and heat to 300°F (150°C). Add garlic slices and fry until slices are completely dry, golden brown, and crisp (at least 3–5 minutes). Remove, drain on paper towel, and let cool. Sprinkle with salt. Store in an airtight container.

Makes about ½ cup (125 ml) chips.

Index